Portraits of the
Archbishops of Canterbury

Portraits of the Archbishops of Canterbury

EDITED BY G. M. BEVAN
AND ISSUED WITH THE APPROVAL OF HIS GRACE
THE ARCHBISHOP OF CANTERBURY

A. R. MOWBRAY & CO. LTD.
LONDON: 34 Great Castle Street, Oxford Circus, W.
OXFORD: 106 S. Aldate's Street
1908

MY DEAR MISS BEVAN,

I cordially approve of your plan of publishing a series of such portraits as exist of the successive occupants of the See of Canterbury.

I gather that you propose to accompany the plates with such biographical notes as may present the facts in outline to those who have little knowledge of English Church History.

I need hardly say that so far as Lambeth is concerned we offer you every facility for the reproduction of pictures or seals.

Such a book as you contemplate will have a peculiar interest this year, when the See of Canterbury forms the pivot of a world-wide gathering.

I am,

Yours very truly,

(*Signed*) RANDALL CANTUAR.

PREFACE

THE idea of this book was suggested by the Guardroom at Lambeth, round which hang the portraits of Archbishops of Canterbury from Arundel to Longley, the series being complete from Warham onwards. In the gallery leading to the Guardroom are the portraits of the three last Archbishops, the picture of Dunstan, and the miniature of Sancroft, a case containing archiepiscopal coins, and another case containing the impressions made from archiepiscopal seals. In the absence of any reliable portraits before the time of Warham, the earlier Archbishops can only be represented by the effigies on their tombs, coins, and seals, and by such pictures as those of Dunstan and Arundel, which, though of very doubtful authenticity as portraits, are included since they form part of the collection at Lambeth. The picture of Alphege is taken from an illuminated MS. by Osbern, who wrote within eighty years of the Archbishop's death.

In order to increase the historical interest of the series, pictures of existing tombs are here reproduced, even when they bear no effigy, but there still remain a large number of Archbishops of whom no sort of representation is possible, and whose tombs no longer exist. It is only by means of the biographical notes that the series can be made so complete as to present an uninterrupted retrospect of the continuity of the Anglican Church extending from our own time through the thirteen centuries which have lapsed since the coming of Augustine. Cursory as such a survey must necessarily be, it may suffice to show something of the varying conditions, of the perils from without, and the perplexities and weakness within, amidst which the life of the Church has been maintained, and has gone forth as a life-giving stream to other lands.

Nor is the interest merely an ecclesiastical one. The biographies of the Archbishops show how large and varied a part they have played in the life of the nation, as statesmen, as men of learning, as leaders in movements of social philanthropy; and at a time when there appears to be a disposition to resent ecclesiastical influence in national affairs, it may not be unprofitable to reflect that before any stable form of government was established in England, and during the centuries which have witnessed the growth of British institutions, the Church—by promoting national education, by inculcating self-control and social responsibility, as well as by the individual capacity of many of her leaders—was building up the State.

My sincere thanks are due to the Archbishop, through whose kind permission the publication of the pictures has been made possible; and also to those who have given me valuable assistance in the preparation of some of the biographical notes.

G. M. BEVAN.

May, 1908.

CONTENTS

9 B

CONTENTS *(continued)*

Lambeth Palace

LAMBETH PALACE

(*From an old painting at the Palace*)

Lambeth Palace

For seven centuries Lambeth has been the abode of the Archbishops of Canterbury. The circumstances which led to the acquisition of this site are alluded to in the biographical notice of Archbishop Baldwin.

It is believed that the oldest existing portions are the Crypt, and the Chapel above it which was built by Archbishop Boniface during the latter half of the thirteenth century.

The Water Tower was erected by Archbishop Chicheley. There appears to be no ground for the popular belief that it served as a prison for Lollards.

The staircase turret, by the side of the Water Tower, has till lately been always regarded as of even greater antiquity, but on this point some doubt appears to exist.

The Guardroom (now used as the dining-room) already existed in 1424, and was extensively repaired by Archbishop Howley in 1829.

The present gateway was built between 1486 and 1500 by Cardinal Morton, and bears his name to this day.

Cranmer is said to have erected the small tower at the north-east of the Chapel. The first floor of the tower, now used as an organ-chamber, goes by the name of "Cranmer's Parlour."

Laud built the small tower on the south side of Chicheley's Water Tower.

During the Rebellion the Roundheads imprisoned at

Lambeth a very large number of Royalists and clergy. Bishop Kennet says: "Near a hundred ministers were brought out of the west and clapped up in Lambeth House, where almost all of them were destroyed by a pestilential fever."

To Juxon's munificence the present Great Hall is due, though a hall undoubtedly existed before his time. There it was that the clergy were required to take the oath accepting Henry VIII as the supreme head of the Church; and there a further oath was demanded, not only assigning the Royal succession to the heirs of Anne Boleyn, but declaring the marriage of Catherine invalid from the beginning. For refusing to take that oath Sir Thomas More passed from the Hall of Lambeth to a prison in the Tower.

Juxon found the Palace a heap of ruins after the havoc wrought by the Roundheads. In restoring the Hall he kept as far as possible to the design of the earlier one. It is now the Library of the Palace. The trial of the Bishop of Lincoln was held in the Great Hall, and there also the second and third Lambeth Conferences took place.

The living-rooms were largely rebuilt by Archbishop Howley, and towards this object he contributed no less than £30,000 from his private purse.

Lambeth Palace Chapel

No place is more intimately associated with the history of the English Church than the Chapel of Lambeth Palace. During six centuries it has witnessed the consecration of a larger number of Bishops than any other church in the kingdom. Within these walls over 400 have received their consecration, and many of them have gone forth from that place to plant the standard of the Church in distant lands. Amongst these were William White, Samuel Provoost, and James Madison, the earliest Bishops of the American Church, with the exception of Bishop Seabury; Charles Inglis, the first Bishop for the colonies; Thomas Middleton, the first Bishop for India, and his successor, Reginald Heber; and William Broughton, the first Bishop of Australia.

The Chapel, built by Archbishop Boniface, was beautified by Cardinal Morton, who filled all the windows with stained glass, but when Laud came to Lambeth he found them "shameful to look on, all diversely patched like a poor beggar's coat." So he set to work to restore them as far as possible according to their original design, which represented scenes from the Old and New Testaments, taken in all probability from the *Biblia Pauperum*. He also set up the screen at the western end. On December 18, 1640, after having been committed to the Tower, he was allowed to pay a last visit to Lambeth. He stayed there till the evening, to avoid the gazing of the people. " I went," he says, "to evening prayer in my chappel.

13

The Psalms of the day, Psalms 93 and 94, gave me great comfort. GOD make me worthy of it, and fit to receive it. As I went to my barge, hundreds of my poor neighbours stood there, and prayed for my safety and return to my house, for which I bless GOD and them."

The Chapel was afterwards wrecked and desecrated by the Roundheads. It was restored by Archbishop Juxon, and a lofty groined roof was substituted by Archbishop Howley for the earlier flat ceiling.

The restoration of the windows was carried out by Archbishop Tait, one window being the gift of the American Bishops in commemoration of the Lambeth Conference of 1878. The beautiful marble which forms the floor of the chancel was a gift to the Archbishop and Mrs. Davidson on the occasion of their silver wedding.

Amongst the notable events which have taken place in the Chapel was the appearance of John Wyclif before Archbishop Sudbury, in 1378, to answer a charge of heresy. The proceedings were interrupted by the citizens of London, who forced their way into the Chapel; and a messenger arrived from the Princess of Wales forbidding the condemnation of Wyclif.

Here in the Chapel which had witnessed his consecration, Archbishop Parker directed that he should be buried in an altar-tomb which was placed during his lifetime at the side of the chancel, "directly against his accustomed place of prayer." During the Commonwealth the grave was destroyed, and the remains cast into an outhouse, whence Archbishop Sancroft caused

LAMBETH PALACE CHAPEL (*Looking East*)

LAMBETH PALACE CHAPEL (Looking West)

them to be brought, and buried in the centre of the Chapel, where they now lie.

Before Sancroft's departure from Lambeth, on the day that Tillotson was consecrated to succeed him (Whitsunday, 1691), the Non-jurors met in the Chapel to take part in a solemn Communion, by which they pledged themselves to maintain an independent Church.

The crypt beneath the Chapel was liable to the influx of water from the river before the present embankment was constructed; and in process of time it was blocked up with earth, which has now been cleared out by the care of the present Archbishop.

Portraits

RANDALL THOMAS DAVIDSON
(The present Archbishop)

The present Archbishop

Randall Thomas Davidson,

D.D., LL.D., G.C.V.O.

Born in Edinburgh, 1848.

Educated at Harrow and at Trinity College, Oxford.

Ordained to curacy of Dartford, 1874.

Resident Chaplain and Secretary to Archbishops Tait and Benson, 1877–1883.

Examining Chaplain to Bishop Lightfoot of Durham, 1881–1883.

Dean of Windsor, and Domestic Chaplain to Queen Victoria, 1883–1891.

Bishop of Rochester, 1891–1895.

Bishop of Winchester, 1895–1903.

Archbishop of Canterbury, 1903.

was born in the Ionian Islands (1821), where his father was British Resident in Santa Maura. He was educated at Blundell's School, Tiverton, and at Balliol College, Oxford, of which he became a Fellow and Tutor, from 1842 to 1848. In 1846 he took Orders. From 1848 to 1857 he was employed in the department of the Council of Education, successively as an Examiner in the office, as Principal of Kneller Hall Training College, and as an Inspector, chiefly of Training Colleges. In 1857 began his famous Head Mastership of Rugby School, which lasted till 1869, when Mr. Gladstone nominated him to the Bishopric of Exeter. He continued throughout his career to take an active part in all educational movements, both primary and secondary. He was a strong supporter of voluntary schools, but his interest in educational matters was always from a national as well as from a Church point of view.

His appointment to the Bishopric of Exeter was objected to in some quarters on account of the contribution which he had made to the volume of *Essays and Reviews*, but the suspicion with which he was at first regarded quickly disappeared as he became known in the diocese.

In 1885 he was appointed Bishop of London. Himself a worker of immense industry, his episcopate was characterized throughout by sympathetic recognition of hard work wherever found. In 1896 he was elevated to the Primacy, at the age of seventy-five. As Arch-

FREDERICK TEMPLE

bishop it fell to his lot to officiate at the Thanksgiving Service for Queen Victoria's Diamond Jubilee in 1897, at her burial in 1901, and at the Coronation of King Edward VII in 1902. In the first year of his Primacy he also issued, with the Archbishop of York, the *Responsio* to the papal bull *Apostolicae Curae*, on the validity of Anglican Orders, which had been prepared by Bishops Wordsworth, Creighton, and Stubbs, under the direction of his predecessor; and in the same summer he presided over the fourth Lambeth Conference, held in the 1300th anniversary year of the landing in England of S. Augustine. To the end of his life the Temperance cause shared with education Archbishop Temple's chief interest and enthusiasm. He was a member of the Royal Commission on the Licensing Laws, and a foremost supporter of the work of the Church of England Temperance Society.

In December, 1902, as the Archbishop was speaking in the House of Lords on the Education Bill of that year, his strength gave way, and within three weeks his strenuous life was brought to a close.

Edward White Benson

was born at Birmingham in 1829, and educated at King
Edward's School in that city, and Trinity College, Cam-
bridge, where he was elected a Fellow. He became
Assistant Master at Rugby, and was ordained in 1853.
Six years later he was appointed the first Head Master
of Wellington College, which he established in the front
rank of English public schools. He became Canon and
Chancellor of Lincoln in 1872.

When the Bishopric of Truro was founded, he
was consecrated as the first Bishop (1877), and the
foundation of the Cathedral was largely due to his
efforts.

In 1883 he was translated to Canterbury. He took
a leading part in ecclesiastical legislation, and was
successful in resisting the attempt to disestablish the
Church in Wales. He showed a deep interest in the
work of foreign Churches, and founded the Mission to
the Assyrian Christians.

The trial of the Bishop of Lincoln for alleged ritual
offences took place in 1888-9, and the Archbishop's
Judgement, delivered in 1890, was considered a master-
piece of ability and learning.

In the course of his life he published several volumes
of Sermons and Charges, and a book on the place and
function of Cathedrals in the work and life of the Church,
but the greater part of his scanty leisure was given, for
nearly thirty years, to the composition of a book entitled
Cyprian, his Life, his Times, his Work which was just

EDWARD WHITE BENSON

completed at the time of his death, and was published posthumously.

Archbishop Benson was pre-eminently a founder and an organizer. Both at Lincoln and Truro he instituted divinity schools for training candidates for Holy Orders, and he built and set in working the only English Cathedral erected in modern times.

He was a man of strong vitality, a fervent idealist, a hard worker, and he had a wide range of interests; but he was pre-eminently an ecclesiastic by instinct and temperament, a born teacher and leader of men, rather than a statesman or a religious philosopher; a restorer and an inspirer, rather than a reformer; by temperament he was sensitive, with a buoyancy and hopefulness that carried him forward, not without despondent reactions. He was generous and large-minded; but yet perhaps owed his success to the fact that his tolerance was limited by marked directness and distinctness of view.

His death occurred suddenly on October 11, 1896, in Hawarden Church, while the guest of Mr. Gladstone. He was buried in the nave of Canterbury Cathedral.

Archibald Campbell Tait

was born at Edinburgh in 1811, and educated at Edinburgh, at Glasgow University, and at Balliol College. He was ordained in 1836, and in addition to a Fellowship and Tutorship of Balliol, undertook the duty of Curate of Marsh Baldon, near Oxford. He was one of the four Tutors who in 1841 protested against Tract XC. In 1842 he succeeded Dr. Arnold as Head Master of Rugby, and in 1849 he became Dean of Carlisle. In 1856 an epidemic of scarlet fever carried off his five little daughters in the course of a few weeks. He was shortly afterwards nominated, on the recommendation of Lord Palmerston, to the See of London. In that diocese he inaugurated evangelistic work in the poorest regions of the metropolis, and founded the Bishop of London's Fund. In 1868 he was promoted to the See of Canterbury.

His political influence was considerable, and he was a great figure in the civic and social life of the nation as well as in the life of the Church. In the House of Lords he took a leading part in the modification of the Bill for the Disestablishment of the Church of Ireland. He is held responsible for the Public Worship Regulation Act of 1874, although its ultimate provisions were altogether different from his original inception and design.

He deprecated any movement which he considered would tend to narrow the limits of that which should be a National Church. He declined to join in the protest

ARCHIBALD CAMPBELL TAIT

against Dr. Hampden's appointment to the Bishopric of Hereford, or in the outcry against Bishop Colenso. The same considerations governed the support which he gave, in the face of much clerical opposition, to the Burials Act of 1880.

In 1867 he had taken a prominent part in the first Lambeth Conference, and it was in great part due to his active promotion and successful Presidency of the second Lambeth Conference, in 1878, that the future of these gatherings became an assured one.

During the last years of his life, in which his home was again clouded by bereavement, he was to a great extent occupied with the work of the Cathedrals Commission, and the Ecclesiastical Courts Commission, and in efforts, rewarded with some success, to compose the growing differences on ritual matters, which he regretted above all as disturbing the peace of the Church, and hindering her true work.

He died on Advent Sunday, 1882.

Archbishop Tait had a large, tranquil, and generous nature. He was tolerant and hopeful, and never afraid to wait. He was a remarkable mixture of shrewdness and simplicity. His energy was calm and constant, rather than impetuous or impassioned; yet he was a man of deep piety, with great reserves of tenderness and loyalty, and with a faith at once childlike and manly.

Charles Thomas Longley

was born at Rochester in 1794, and educated at Cheam
School, Westminster School, and Christ Church, Oxford.
He took Holy Orders in 1818, and held the living of
Cowley, and then of West Tytherley till 1829, when
he was elected Head Master of Harrow. He was appointed first Bishop of Ripon in 1836. His tenure of
that See was marked by his personal vigour, and the
stable foundation which he laid for Church work and
life in the West Riding of Yorkshire. He became
successively Bishop of Durham, Archbishop of York,
and in 1862 Archbishop of Canterbury.

His Primacy was marked by two great controversies,
that over the prosecutions of some of the contributors
to the volume of *Essays and Reviews*, and that over
Bishop Colenso's writings. In the latter case, Archbishop Longley on the whole shared the view of those
who held that Colenso had been rightly deposed from
the Bishopric of Natal.

Under Longley's Presidency the first Lambeth
Conference, attended by seventy-eight British, Colonial,
American, and Missionary Bishops, was held at Lambeth in 1867, to promote a truer union of work throughout the scattered branches of the Anglican Church.

Longley died in 1868.

CHARLES THOMAS LONGLEY

JOHN BIRD SUMNER

John Bird Sumner

was born at Kenilworth in 1780, and educated at Eton, and King's College, Cambridge. He was ordained in 1802, and was appointed to a Prebendal stall at Durham Cathedral in 1820. In 1828 he became Bishop of Chester, and displayed great energy in providing new churches and schools throughout his diocese. In 1848 he was promoted to the See of Canterbury.

He had voted in favour of the Reform Bill in 1832, and he also voted for the repeal of the disabilities imposed on Roman Catholics, although he opposed the Bill for removing Jewish disabilities. He concurred in the decision of the Privy Council with regard to the Rev. G. C. Gorham, who had been charged with holding heretical views on the subject of Holy Baptism.

In 1852 Convocation met for the first time after a lapse of one hundred and thirty-five years.

Archbishop Sumner published numerous works, including sermons and theological treatises, and several volumes of *Expositions of the New Testament*, which had a wide circulation.

His death took place in 1862.

William Howley

son of a Hampshire clergyman, was born in 1766. He was educated at Winchester, and New College, of which he became a Fellow and Tutor, and he was also elected a Fellow of Winchester. He was appointed in 1796 to the Vicarage of Bishops Sutton, and subsequently held the livings of Andover and Bradford Peverell. From 1809 he was Regius Professor of Divinity at Oxford until 1813, when he was appointed Bishop of London. He was translated to Canterbury in 1828, and in this capacity, on the morning of June 20, 1837, he accompanied the Lord Chamberlain to Kensington Palace, to announce to Queen Victoria her accession to the throne.

The twenty years of Howley's Primacy, from 1828 to 1848, were years of considerable development of life and activity in the Church both at home and abroad. The Ecclesiastical Commission was founded in 1836, as the result of a Royal Commission appointed in 1831 to report upon the exact condition of ecclesiastical revenues, the Archbishop cordially co-operating with the Whig Government of the day in the new departure which made it possible to apply the residue of the estates of Bishops and Cathedral bodies to the augmentation of poor livings, and the endowment of new parishes in populous districts. In 1838 and in 1841 were passed the Act for abolishing pluralities and non-residence, and the Church Discipline Act. In 1841 the Colonial Bishoprics Fund was started as the outcome of a meeting presided over by the Archbishop. To Howley's Primacy also belongs the beginning of the Oxford Movement. Its closing years witnessed the earlier ritual controversies.

Archbishop Howley was a great builder. As Bishop of London, he rebuilt London House, and restored Fulham Palace. As Archbishop he rebuilt the later dwelling parts of Lambeth Palace. He died in 1848.

WILLIAM HOWLEY

CHARLES MANNERS SUTTON

Charles Manners Sutton

was born in 1755, and educated at Charterhouse, and Emmanuel College, Cambridge. He was given the benefices of Whitwell and Averham-with-Kelham, and the Deanery of Peterborough, and in 1792 became Bishop of Norwich. He was also made Dean of Windsor, and in 1805 was translated to the See of Canterbury.

As Archbishop he showed active sympathy with the movement for the revival of Church life. The founding of the National Society was largely due to his efforts. The persevering endeavours of the Society for Promoting Christian Knowledge to establish an episcopate in India were at last rewarded in 1814, when the first Bishop of Calcutta was consecrated in the Chapel of Lambeth Palace.

Archbishop Manners Sutton died in 1828.

John Moore

the son of a Gloucestershire grazier, was born in 1730, and educated at Gloucester Grammar School, and Pembroke College, Oxford, and became a tutor in the house of the Duke of Marlborough. He was given a Prebend at Durham and a Canonry at Oxford, was made Dean of Canterbury, and in 1775 became Bishop of Bangor. He succeeded to the Primacy in 1783.

He was a warm supporter and promoter of the Sunday School movement; he co-operated with Wilberforce in his efforts for association to promote " a reformation of manners," and he furthered the work of Foreign Missions.

It was during his Primacy that the first Bishop of the American Church—Bishop Seabury—was consecrated in Scotland in 1786, and in the following year two more American Bishops, Bishops White and Provoost, and the first Bishop for the Colonies, Bishop Inglis of Nova Scotia, were consecrated by Moore himself in Lambeth Palace Chapel.

He died in 1805.

JOHN MOORE

(By Romney)

FREDERICK CORNWALLIS

Frederick Cornwallis

was born in 1713, and was educated at Eton, and Christ's College, Cambridge. He held the livings of Chelmondiston, and Tittleshall S. Mary, and became one of the King's Chaplains-in-Ordinary, and Canon of Windsor.

In 1750 he was consecrated Bishop of Coventry and Lichfield, and translated to Canterbury in 1768, in succession to Archbishop Secker. His tenure of the Primacy was uneventful, but evidence has come down in contemporary letters and journals of his personal kindness to his clergy, and of his wide and tolerant views on public questions.

His death took place in 1783.

Thomas Secker

was born in Nottinghamshire in 1693, and was brought up as a Dissenter. He was educated at the school kept by Samuel Jones, first at Gloucester, and then at Tewkesbury. There he made the acquaintance of Joseph Butler, afterwards Bishop of Durham, and it was largely due to him and to Martin Benson, who was afterwards Bishop of Gloucester, that Secker was led to abandon the study of medicine, and to enter Exeter College, Oxford, with the view of taking Holy Orders. After his ordination in 1722 he was given the living of Houghton-le-Spring, and later a Prebend at Durham, and the Rectory of S. James's, Piccadilly, and he was also Chaplain to the King. In 1735 he was consecrated Bishop of Bristol, became Bishop of Oxford two years later, and Dean of S. Paul's in 1750. In 1758 he succeeded to the Primacy.

The neglected condition of the Colonies was to him a source of much concern, and he ardently desired that bishoprics should be established in America. Yet even the proposal that " two or three persons should be ordained Bishops, and sent to our American Colonies," met with so much opposition that it could not be carried out in his lifetime.

His death took place in 1768.

THOMAS SECKER
(By Sir Joshua Reynolds)

MATTHEW HUTTON

Matthew Hutton

was born in Yorkshire in 1693, and educated at Kirby Hill, Ripon, and Jesus College, Cambridge. He became Fellow of Christ's College, Rector of Trowbridge, Rector of Spofforth, Prebendary of York, and Chaplain to George II. In 1737 he was appointed to a Canonry at Windsor, which he exchanged two years later for a Prebend at Westminster. He was consecrated Bishop of Bangor in 1743, was translated to York in 1747, and to Canterbury in 1757.

His tenure of the Primacy lasted less than a year, and he never actually resided at Lambeth.

Thomas Herring

was born in Norfolk in 1693, and educated at Wisbech, and Jesus College, Cambridge. He was elected to a Fellowship at Corpus Christi College, and took Orders in 1716. He held the livings of Rettendon and Barley, and afterwards of Bletchingley, and was appointed Preacher at Lincoln's Inn, and Chaplain to the King, and Dean of Rochester. In 1738 he became Bishop of Bangor, and five years later Archbishop of York. While at York, Herring, who was a wholehearted supporter of the House of Hanover, took a leading part during the Rebellion of 1745 in forming an association "for the defence of the constitution and liberties of the kingdom."

He was translated to Canterbury in 1747, and died in 1757. As a younger man he was noted as a preacher.

The period of the Primacy of Herring and his immediate successors was one in which the Church of England was lacking in life and energy, and most of the religious zeal and fervour of the nation found its outlet outside the borders of the National Church.

THOMAS HERRING
(By Hogarth)

JOHN POTTER

John Potter

was born about 1674 at Wakefield, where he was educated, and then proceeded to University College, Oxford. He became Fellow of Lincoln College, and took Orders in 1698, and was Chaplain to Archbishop Tenison till his appointment to the Regius Professorship of Divinity at Oxford. In 1715 he was appointed Bishop of Oxford, and in 1737 succeeded to the Primacy.

His attitude to some of the religious movements of his day is indicated by his recognition of the good work done by the Methodist preachers, and by the cordial letter he addressed to Count Zinzendorf on his consecration as Bishop of the Moravian Church.

Archbishop Potter died in 1747.

William Wake

was born in 1657 at Blandford, where he was educated till he entered Christ Church, Oxford. For three years he lived in Paris as Chaplain to the English Ambassador, Lord Preston; and after his return to England he was appointed Preacher of Gray's Inn, Chaplain-in-Ordinary to William and Mary, Canon of Christ Church, Rector of S. James's, Westminster, and Dean of Exeter. In 1705 he became Bishop of Lincoln, and was raised to the Primacy in 1716.

A communication was addressed to him by certain members of the Gallican Church who were dissatisfied with the extreme papal claims, and who were desirous of coming into closer relation with the Anglican Church. The Archbishop was very favourably disposed to the scheme, and negotiations were carried on for some time in the hope of effecting a reunion, but eventually they proved fruitless.

Archbishop Wake was the author of numerous works, chiefly relating to the history of the Church.

His death occurred in 1737.

WILLIAM WAKE

THOMAS TENISON

Thomas Tenison

was born in 1636 at Cottenham. He was educated at Norwich, and Corpus Christi College, Cambridge, and became Fellow of his College, and Tutor. After holding the livings of S. Andrew the Great, Cambridge, and Holywell and Needingworth, he was appointed to the Rectory of S. Martin in the Fields, where he showed great activity as a controversialist, but at the same time he maintained a conciliatory attitude towards Dissenters. He enjoyed the confidence of William III, and was presented by him to the Archdeaconry of London. In 1692 he became Bishop of Lincoln, and three years later was translated to Canterbury. During Queen Anne's reign he used his influence to secure the succession of George I.

Archbishop Tenison, by his active interest and his liberal gifts, gave strong support to works of philanthropy, and founded a school at his own expense. In 1701 he took part in drawing up a charter for founding the Society for the Propagation of the Gospel in Foreign Parts; he was the first contributor towards the charges of passing the charter, and became the first President of the new Society. By his will he bequeathed £1,000 towards providing Bishops for the American Colonies.

He died in 1715.

was born at Halifax in 1630, and is said to have been educated at Colne, and the Heath Grammar School at Halifax, and then entered Clare Hall, Cambridge, where he obtained a Fellowship. He became Rector of Kedington, and Preacher at Lincoln's Inn, and frequently lectured at S. Lawrence Jewry.

He was a diligent student of the Bible, and of the early Fathers, and bestowed great care upon the preparation and delivery of his sermons, which produced an extraordinary impression by the freshness of their appeal to reason and feeling. The title of one of his sermons—"The Wisdom of being Religious"—may indicate their special character. His preaching was considered very effective against Popery, and it was not altogether to the taste of the Puritans. At the same time, Tillotson manifested throughout his career a disposition to grant a large toleration to Dissenters, and thought that they might be conciliated if concessions were made to them.

He was made Chaplain to Charles II, who gave him the Deanery of Canterbury. In 1688 he took part in the deliberations which led Sancroft and six other Bishops to draw up their remonstrance to James II on his attempt to procure their agreement to his "Declaration of Indulgence."

Upon the accession of William III he became Dean of S. Paul's, and was appointed to exercise archiepiscopal jurisdiction owing to the suspension of Sancroft. It

JOHN TILLOTSON

was the wish of William that he should become Primate, but he was so reluctant to be made "a wedge to drive out" Sancroft that his consecration did not take place till 1691.

He warmly supported missionary effort, and the religious societies which were formed to promote devotion and benevolence.

His attempt to reform certain abuses in the Church, and especially non-residence among the clergy, aroused much ill-will, of which his enemies were not slow to take advantage. This, though it "could neither provoke him nor fright him from his duty, affected his mind so much that it was thought to have shortened his days."

His death took place in 1694.

was born in Suffolk in 1617, and educated at Bury
S. Edmunds, and Emmanuel College, Cambridge.
After the Restoration he was given the Rectory of
Houghton-le-Spring, became Chaplain to the King, was
made Master of his College, and Dean of York, and in
1664 was nominated to the Deanery of S. Paul's.   He
spared neither time nor expense in rebuilding the
Cathedral after its destruction in the Great Fire.   In
1668 he became Archdeacon of Canterbury, and was
promoted to the Primacy in 1678.

In 1688, James II, who had shown his determination
to set aside the Test Act, issued a declaration revoking
all the disabilities imposed upon Nonconformists, and
commanded that the declaration should be read in every
church throughout the kingdom.   Sancroft, with six
other Bishops, drew up a protest addressed to the King.
The seven Bishops were committed to the Tower, but
their trial resulted in a triumphant acquittal.

In 1690 he was deposed for refusing to take the oath
of allegiance to William and Mary, holding that "as long
as King James was alive no other persons could be
sovereigns of the country."   Five other Non-juring
Bishops and about four hundred clergy were also deprived for the same reason.

From the time that he left Lambeth till his death,
in 1693, he lived in a small house which he had built
at Fressingfield, his native place, and occupied himself
with literary work, and with schemes for maintaining
the succession in the Non-juring body.

WILLIAM SANCROFT

(From a miniature)

GILBERT SHELDON

Gilbert Sheldon

was born in Derbyshire in 1598, and studied at Trinity College, Oxford. He was elected Fellow of All Souls, of which he subsequently became Warden. In 1622 he was ordained, and given a Prebend at Gloucester, and the benefices of Hackney, Oddington, Ickford, and Newington.

As a Royalist and an anti-Puritan he was obnoxious to the Parliamentary party, who ejected him from All Souls in 1648, but he was reinstated in 1659. At the Restoration he became Dean of the Chapel Royal, and Bishop of London, and succeeded Archbishop Juxon at Canterbury in 1663.

He was elected Chancellor of the University of Oxford, and at his own charges built the theatre there known as the Sheldonian.

He was distinguished no less for his faithfulness to the duties of his high office than for his great munificence. Whilst the Plague was at its height he remained at Lambeth to succour the sufferers; and he forfeited the favour of Charles II by his boldness in reproving him for his evil life.

He also took an active interest in the work of the Church in other lands.

His death took place in 1677.

William Juxon

was born at Chichester, and educated at the Merchant
Taylors' School, and then proceeded to S. John's College,
Oxford, where he studied law. After his ordination, in
1609, he held the living of S. Giles', Oxford, and then of
Somerton. He was elected to the Presidency of S. John's
College, and became Chaplain-in-Ordinary to the King.
In 1626 he was appointed Vice-Chancellor of the Uni-
versity, and Dean of Worcester; and in 1633, on Laud's
recommendation, he was consecrated Bishop of London,
in which capacity he was distinguished for his clemency.
He also received the office of Lord High Treasurer, and
Lord of the Admiralty.

King Charles held him in high esteem, and he alone
stood by the King in his last hour on the scaffold, and
bade him farewell with the words: "You are exchanged
from a temporal to an eternal crown, a good exchange."
He was deprived of his See in 1649, but at the Restoration was nominated to the Primacy.

He restored S. Paul's Cathedral, and rebuilt the Great
Hall at Lambeth.

He died in 1663.

WILLIAM JUXON

WILLIAM LAUD

(By Vandyck)

William Laud

was born in 1573 at Reading, where he received his early education. He then entered S. John's College, Oxford, and obtained a Fellowship, and was elected President of S. John's in 1611. He became Archdeacon of Huntingdon, and Dean of Gloucester, and in 1621 was appointed to the Bishopric of S. David's. Five years later he was translated to Bath and Wells, and appointed Dean of the Chapel Royal, and a Privy Councillor. He became Bishop of London in 1628, and the following year he was elected Chancellor of the University of Oxford. His elevation to the Primacy took place in 1633. He states that at the same time he received the offer of a Cardinal's hat, "but my answer was that somewhat dwelt within me, which would not suffer that till Rome were other than it is."

From the outset of his career Laud had been regarded with suspicion by the Puritan party, which was strongly imbued with the views of Continental Protestantism. Laud, on the other hand, was resolutely determined to maintain the historic continuity of the English Church, to permit no breach of her constitution, and no departure from her teaching. With absolute honesty of purpose and perfect fearlessness he directed his energies to quell the forces of ecclesiastical disorder, thinking to achieve his end by a rigorous assertion of authority. Yet beneath this unyielding exterior there dwelt a fervent piety, and a deep humility which appeared in the manner in which he endured the personal insults which were heaped upon him, and which he keenly felt.

His attachment to the King, and his position as an adviser to the Crown, increased his unpopularity with those who were dissatisfied with the government of Charles, and in 1640 he was accused of high treason by the House of Commons, and committed to the Tower a few months later. The trial did not begin till 1644, and it was conducted with hardly a semblance of justice. Laud was charged with the attempt to subvert the laws of the kingdom, and to bring in Popery. No accusation could be proved against him, but he was condemned to death.

He suffered on Tower Hill, January 10, 1645.

GEORGE ABBOT

George Abbot

was born in 1562 at Guildford, where he was educated before entering Balliol College, Oxford. He gained a great reputation at Oxford as an advocate of the views held by the more moderate Puritans, and was elected Master of University College, Dean of Winchester, and Vice-Chancellor of the University.

In 1604 he was engaged upon the new translation of the Bible. He accompanied Lord Dunbar to Scotland in 1608, with the view of restoring the Scottish episcopate. The following year he became Bishop of Coventry and Lichfield, and a few months later was translated to the Bishopric of London. His elevation to the Primacy followed in 1611.

Abbot was a man of strong principles, but narrow outlook. He could act with great firmness when he felt conscientiously obliged to follow a difficult course, as in the case of Lady Essex's divorce, yet he was strangely unwilling to allow to others liberty of conscience, and he sought to suppress opinions which he disliked by measures of excessive harshness. His aversion to Popery was such that he was even ready to foment a war with Spain. On the other hand, he addressed some separatists who were brought before him with great severity: "You do show yourselves the most ungrateful to GOD, to the King, and to us the fathers of the Church."

In 1621 he had the misfortune to shoot a keeper at a hunting party. It was clear that the Archbishop was in no way to blame for the accident, but it afforded his enemies a fresh ground of attack, and it cast a cloud over his latter years.

Abbot found little favour in the eyes of Charles I and his advisers. A feud had existed between Abbot and Laud from early days. In 1627 he was suspended from the exercise of his archiepiscopal functions, and the sequestration lasted for more than a year.

Notwithstanding the sternness of his disposition, he showed great liberality in the relief of individual cases of distress, and in other benefactions, especially to Oxford Colleges, and to the hospital which he had built at Guildford.

He died in 1633.

RICHARD BANCROFT

Richard Bancroft

was born in 1544 at Farnworth, in Lancashire, where he was educated before he proceeded to Christ's College, Cambridge. He afterwards entered Jesus College, became Chaplain to the Bishop of Ely, and was given the living of Teversham, and then of Cottingham, was appointed Treasurer of S. Paul's, a member of the Ecclesiastical Commission, and Canon of Westminster. In 1592 he became Chaplain to Archbishop Whitgift, and was promoted to the See of London in 1597. He was distinguished for the zeal with which he opposed Puritanism, notably at the Hampton Court Conference (1604).

The same year he was translated to Canterbury, and gave strong support to the scheme for a new translation of the Bible. In 1608 he was elected Chancellor of the University of Oxford. He sought to promote scholarship amongst the clergy, and bequeathed to his successors in the See of Canterbury his collection of books, which formed the foundation of the Lambeth Library.

He died in 1610.

John Whitgift

was born at Great Grimsby, and was educated at
S. Anthony's School, in London, and then at Queen's
College and Pembroke Hall, Cambridge. He took
Orders in 1560, was appointed to the Rectory of Tever-
sham, and in 1563 became Lady Margaret Professor of
Divinity, which he resigned for the Regius Professorship
of Divinity. He was made Master of Trinity College,
Chaplain to Queen Elizabeth, Vice-Chancellor of the
University of Cambridge, and Dean of Lincoln. In
1577 he was consecrated to the Bishopric of Worcester,
and in 1583 was translated to Canterbury.

Whilst at Cambridge he had devoted himself with
great vigour to his academic duties. The same zeal was
displayed during his episcopate in the government of the
Church, and more especially in the stern measures which
he conceived it to be his duty to take for the suppression
of Puritanism. It was during his archiepiscopate that
the Hampton Court Conference met (1604).

As he lay dying, a few weeks later, words were con-
stantly on his lips which well sum up the purpose of his
life: *Pro ecclesia Dei.*

JOHN WHITGIFT

EDMUND GRINDAL

Edmund Grindal

was born in Cumberland about 1519, and was educated at Magdalene College, Christ's College, and Pembroke Hall, Cambridge, and became Chaplain to Bishop Ridley, Chaplain to the King, and Prebendary of Westminster. During the reign of Queen Mary he lived abroad. On his return to England he was appointed Master of Pembroke Hall, and Bishop of London. In 1562 he took part in revising the Articles of Religion. Not being found resolute enough to cope with Puritanism in the Diocese of London, he was appointed Archbishop of York in 1570. In 1576, on Cecil's recommendation, he was translated to Canterbury, but soon came into conflict with the Queen, who desired him to suppress the meetings called " prophesyings," which were chiefly attended by the Puritan clergy. Upon Grindal's refusal, he was suspended from his functions in 1577, nor was he fully reinstated till 1582, when he had expressed regret for offending the Queen.

The following year he died.

Matthew Parker

was born at Norwich in 1504, and was educated at
S. Mary's Hostel, and Corpus Christi College, Cambridge. He was ordained in 1527, and was appointed
Dean of the College of S. John the Baptist at Stoke-by-
Clare, and Chaplain to Anne Boleyn and to the King.
In 1544 he was elected Master of his College at Cambridge, and Vice-Chancellor of the University; and upon
the accession of Elizabeth he took part in the revision
of the Prayer Book. He was consecrated Archbishop
of Canterbury in Lambeth Palace Chapel in 1559.

The Anglican Church owes much to the wisdom and
judgement with which Parker guided her course through
a time of great difficulty, when she was in peril from the
Roman party on the one hand, and the Puritans on the
other. His devotion to the cause of learning was shown
by the magnificent collection of books which he made
and bequeathed to his College, and by the publication
of the " Bishops' Bible "; and he was himself the author
of various works, chiefly on the history and the government of the Anglican Church.

He died in 1575.

MATTHEW PARKER

REGINALD POLE

grandson of George, Duke of Clarence, was born in Staffordshire (1500), and educated at the school of the Charterhouse at Sheen, and the house of the Carmelite Friars, Oxford. He matriculated at Magdalen College, and became Dean of Wimborne Minster, and afterwards Dean of Exeter. He studied in Italy and France, and as he was known to be opposed to the King's divorce, and to his anti-papal policy, he deemed it wiser to remain abroad. In 1536 he was summoned to Rome by Paul III, who insisted that he should take Deacon's Orders, and be made a Cardinal. In the following year he was appointed Legate. He was present at the opening of the Council of Trent, and he was employed by the Pope in missions to the King of France and other princes with the view of forcibly restoring the papal authority in England. Failure attended his efforts. His mother was brought to the block, and his own attainder soon followed. The accession of Queen Mary in 1553 changed the aspect of affairs. Pole returned to England, and became Primate in 1556. But his long services to the Papacy were not destined to be crowned with any lasting success. His friend, Paul III, had died in 1549, and Paul IV regarded him with dislike and suspicion. Having plunged into a war with Spain, he withdrew his Legates from all parts of Philip's dominions, and though Pole was desirous of remaining neutral, he found himself suspected of heresy, and deprived of his legatine office at a time when he had special need of the authority which it conferred upon him. In consequence of his remonstrance, the Pope appears eventually to have yielded so far as to allow him to retain his position as Legate.

Pole was spared the mortification of witnessing the final overthrow of the papal domination in England which followed the death of Queen Mary, for he survived the Queen but a few hours, dying on November 17, 1558.

THOMAS CRANMER

Thomas Cranmer

was born in Nottinghamshire in 1489, and was educated at Cambridge, and in 1530 became Archdeacon of Taunton. The course which he advocated with regard to the divorce of Queen Catherine brought him into favour with Henry VIII, and in 1533 he was appointed Archbishop of Canterbury.

The servility with which Cranmer lent himself to the accomplishment of Henry's lawless desires, the timidity which made him acquiesce in deeds of tyranny and violence, from which his conscience revolted, remain as a blot on his memory. Yet it was in great measure due to him that the English Church emerged from the fierce ordeal retaining unimpaired her ancient Faith and Apostolic succession. The Book of Common Prayer is the lasting memorial of the religious spirit of that time, and Cranmer is entitled to the fullest share of praise for the wisdom which guided its compilation. The Sarum Use, which had acquired a dominant position in the English Church in mediæval times, was retained, with certain alterations, as the groundwork of the book, and this was enriched by contributions from very varied sources. The first Prayer Book appeared in 1549. Under the stress of foreign influences it was subjected to certain alterations in 1552, but these were again considerably modified in the direction of the earlier book in 1559.

When Edward VI was dying, Cranmer was persuaded, much against his will, to sign the document by which the King designated Lady Jane Grey as his successor. After the failure of the attempt to place her on the throne, Cranmer was charged with treason and sedition, and committed to the Tower. Thence he was taken to Oxford, and required to defend himself against the charge of heresy. Finally sentence of death by burning was passed upon him. In the hope of saving his life he recanted his opinions, but when called upon to disavow them openly, he expressed deep regret for the cowardice which had led to his recantation, and went courageously to his death (1556).

WILLIAM WARHAM
(By Holbein)

William Warham

born about 1450, was educated at Winchester, and New College, Oxford. He became an advocate in the Court of Arches, Principal of the Civil Law School at Oxford, and Master of the Rolls. He also held the livings of Barley and Cottenham, and was appointed Precentor of Wells, and Archdeacon of Huntingdon. In 1496 he conducted the negotiations for the marriage of Prince Arthur with Catherine of Arragon, and was employed from the outset of his career in many diplomatic missions, which led him to visit Flanders, France, Scotland, and perhaps Rome. He became Bishop of London, and Keeper of the Great Seal in 1502, which title he exchanged for that of Lord Chancellor when he was promoted to the Primacy in 1503. Though he resigned the Great Seal to Wolsey in 1515, he continued to take a leading part in the affairs of State.

When the King was seeking a divorce, Warham was appointed counsel to Queen Catherine, but he showed himself unable to oppose Henry's wishes. Nor was he able to offer any effectual resistance when the King, having compelled the clergy to acknowledge the Royal supremacy, demanded the further surrender of their independence, known as "the submission of the clergy."

Warham was for many years Chancellor of the University of Oxford, at a time when the revival of letters had invested Oxford with a new glory. No one showed a more generous appreciation of the New Learning. He delighted in the society of scholars, and promoted literary enterprises with a splendid liberality. Erasmus became his friend, and not only received much personal kindness from the Archbishop, but was enabled by his help to produce his famous Greek Testament.

Warham died in 1532.

Henry Dean

of whose early life nothing is known, was Prior of the house of Augustine Canons at Llanthony. He became the trusted adviser of Henry VII, who appointed him Chancellor of Ireland in 1494, and sent him to establish order in that country. Dean had been elected to the Bishopric of Bangor before he left England, and after two years in Ireland, he took possession of his See, and devoted himself with much energy to restoring the Cathedral and the Bishop's Palace, which had been destroyed by Owen Glendower. In 1500 he was translated to Salisbury, and soon after became Keeper of the Great Seal, and Archbishop of Canterbury (1501). The same year he headed the commission appointed to arrange the marriage of Princess Margaret with James IV of Scotland, and signed a treaty of perpetual peace between the two countries.

He died in 1503.

TOMB OF JOHN MORTON
(In Canterbury Cathedral)

John Morton

was born in Dorset about 1420, and educated at Cerne Abbey, and Balliol College.   He took Orders, and became an ecclesiastical lawyer in the Court of Arches.   He was appointed a member of the Privy Council, Chancellor of the Duchy of Cornwall, and Master in Chancery.

During the Wars of the Roses he cast in his lot with the Lancastrians, and was involved in their misfortunes, but on making his submission, he was received into favour by Edward IV, and was employed by him on diplomatic missions.

He was made Archdeacon of Winchester and of Chester in 1474, and Bishop of Ely in 1479.

He was imprisoned by Richard III, but escaped to Flanders, and was thence recalled by Henry VII, whose financial minister and adviser he became.   In 1486 he was made Archbishop of Canterbury, and Lord Chancellor, was created a Cardinal in 1493, and elected Chancellor of the University of Oxford in 1495.

His death took place in 1500.

Morton was a great builder.   The central tower of Canterbury Cathedral, known both as the " Angel Steeple," and as " Bell Harry," erected by Prior Goldstone with Morton's help and at his expense, and the Gateway Tower of Lambeth Palace, where he lived and where Sir Thomas More served him as page, and which bears his name, remain as monuments of his taste and munificence.

Thomas Bourchier

was born about 1404, his mother being the grand-daughter of Edward III. He went to Oxford, and took up his residence at Nevill's Inn.

He early obtained several preferments, amongst them being the Deanery of S. Martin's-le-Grand, London. In 1434 he also became Chancellor of the University of Oxford. In the following year he was made Bishop of Worcester, and in 1443 was translated to Ely. His elevation to the Primacy took place eleven years later, and it was soon followed by his appointment as Lord Chancellor.

When the Wars of the Roses broke out, Bourchier attempted for a time to mediate between the two parties. Finally, he placed himself on the side of the Yorkists, and officiated at the Coronation of Edward IV. In 1471, together with other peers of the realm, he took an oath accepting the Prince of Wales as heir to the throne, but at the death of Edward IV his son was set aside, and Bourchier placed the crown on the head of Richard III.

The closing scene of his public life was in 1486, when the strife between the red rose and the white was ended by the marriage of Henry VII and Elizabeth of York.

Bourchier's death took place in 1486.

TOMB OF THOMAS BOURCHIER
(In Canterbury Cathedral)

TOMB OF JOHN KEMP

(In Canterbury Cathedral)

John Kemp

was born near Ashford, and educated at Merton College, Oxford. After having practised as an ecclesiastical lawyer, he became Dean of the Court of Arches, Vicar-General to Archbishop Chicheley, and Keeper of the Privy Seal, and was employed by Henry V to conduct negotiations with Arragon, Sicily, and France.

He was appointed to the Archdeaconry of Durham, and in 1419 became Bishop of Rochester, being translated in 1421 to the See of Chichester, and during the same year to London. He was a member of the Council which was appointed after the accession of Henry VI, and in 1426 became both Chancellor and Archbishop of York. Kemp was too much engrossed with his political duties to devote much attention to the administration of his diocese, in which great disorder prevailed.

He exerted himself to bring the war with France to a close, and took a leading part in the embassies which attempted, without success, to negotiate a peace; and he was the mainstay of the Lancastrian party.

In 1439 he was created a Cardinal by Eugenius IV, and was translated to the See of Canterbury in 1452.

His death took place in 1454.

John Stafford

studied law at Oxford, and was appointed Dean of the
Court of Arches, Archdeacon and Chancellor of Salis-
bury, Dean of S. Martin's, London, Dean of Wells,
Keeper of the Privy Seal, and Lord High Treasurer.

In 1425 he became Bishop of Bath and Wells, and
for seventeen years held the office of Lord Chancellor.
His political influence was employed on the side of those
who desired to promote peace with France.

Archbishop Chicheley designated Stafford as his
successor, on the ground of " his high intellectual and
moral qualifications, the nobility of his birth, the
influence of his relations, and his own almost boundless
hospitality." Stafford was accordingly translated to
Canterbury in 1443.

He died in 1452.

HENRY CHICHELE.
(From his Tomb in Canterbury Cathedral)

Henry Chicheley

born about 1362, was the son of a yeoman of Higham Ferrers, Northamptonshire. He was educated at Winchester, and New College, Oxford, with which the munificence of William of Wykeham had recently endowed the University.

Chicheley held the living of S. Stephen's, Walbrook, till his appointment to the Archdeaconry of Dorset, and afterwards became Archdeacon of Salisbury, and held Canonries in the Dioceses of Salisbury and Lichfield. He took part in diplomatic missions to France, and to the Popes Innocent VII and Gregory XII.

In 1408 he was consecrated to the Bishopric of S. Davids, and was translated to Canterbury in 1414. He gave his support to King Henry's campaign in France, and was one of the Ambassadors who carried on the negotiations for a truce.

The liberty of the National Church, which was increasingly threatened by papal aggression, found in him a staunch defender. He also occupied himself actively in the administration of his Province, in the suppression of heresy, and in promoting education. All Souls College was founded by him, and at Lambeth he built the tower which erroneously came to be known as the Lollards' Tower.

He died in 1443.

Roger Walden

of whose early life nothing certain is known, held benefices in Jersey, Yorkshire, and Leicester. He was
appointed Archdeacon of Westminster in 1387, and
Treasurer of England in 1395. He was also given
Prebends at Lincoln, Salisbury, Exeter, Lichfield, and
S. Paul's, the Rectory of S. Andrew's, Holborn, and
the Deanery of York. When Archbishop Arundel was
banished in 1398, Walden was promoted to the See of
Canterbury, of which he was deprived at Arundel's
restoration. In 1405 Arundel persuaded Innocent VII
to appoint him to the Bishopric of London.

Though in his early life he had been largely occupied
with secular affairs, he earned respect in his latter years
by his moderation and his devotion to the duties of his
office.

He died in 1406.

THOMAS ARUNDEL

Thomas Arundel

the son of Richard Fitzalan, Earl of Arundel, was promoted at an early age to the Archdeaconry of Taunton, and the Bishopric of Ely. In 1386 the unsettled state of the country and the prevailing discontent led to the appointment of a Commission of Regency, consisting of eleven lords, one of whom was Arundel's brother, whilst Arundel became Chancellor.

In 1388 he succeeded to the Archbishopric of York, and in 1396 he was translated to Canterbury. Seven months later he was impeached by the House of Commons on the charge of having taken part, eleven years previously, in procuring the Commission of Regency to the prejudice of the King. His brother was put to death, and sentence of banishment was passed on the Archbishop.

In 1399 he returned to England with Henry of Bolingbroke, and took part in the proceedings which led to Richard's abdication. He once more took possession of his See, and crowned Henry. During the later years of his life, his attention was mainly directed to the suppression of Lollardism.

He died in 1414.

William Courtenay

son of the Earl of Devon, was born at Exeter about
1342, and studied law at Stapledon Hall, Oxford. He
was elected Chancellor of the University, and held
Prebends at Exeter, Wells, and York. At the age of
twenty-eight he was consecrated Bishop of Hereford,
and six years later became Bishop of London. He took
part with William of Wykeham in defending the rights
of the clergy: on the one hand, against the attacks made
upon them by John of Gaunt, and on the other, against
the exactions of the Pope. In 1381 he was translated
to Canterbury, and exerted himself for the suppression
of Lollardism. Wyclif's opinions were formally condemned at a Council held in his presence at Blackfriars
in 1382.

Courtenay died in 1396 at Maidstone, and is thought
by some to have been buried there, but there is more
reason to believe that his body was transferred to
Canterbury.

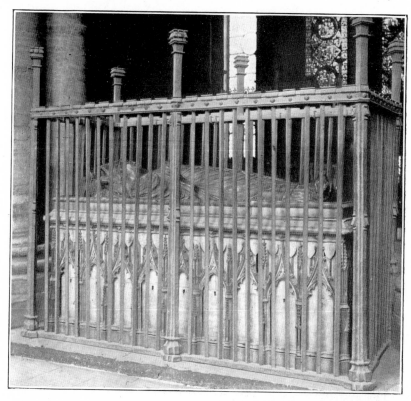

TOMB OF WILLIAM COURTENAY

(In Canterbury Cathedral)

TOMB OF SIMON SUDBURY

(In Canterbury Cathedral)

Simon Sudbury

was born at Sudbury, in Suffolk, and studied law at the University of Paris. He entered the service of Pope Innocent VI, and was promoted by him to the See of London in 1362. He was employed in diplomatic negotiations with France and Flanders. In 1375 he was translated to the See of Canterbury, and in 1378 he cited Wyclif to appear in the Chapel of Lambeth Palace, to answer the charges brought against him.

He began the rebuilding of Canterbury Cathedral, and made large contributions of his own money.

In 1380 he became Chancellor.

When the "Wat Tyler" rising of 1381 took place, the insurgents, at the instigation of the excommunicated priest, John Ball, seized the Archbishop, and beheaded him on Tower Hill.

William Whittlesey

was born in Cambridgeshire, and studied law at Oxford. He held several preferments at Cambridge, Lichfield, Chichester, and Lincoln, besides two benefices, and the Archdeaconry of Huntingdon. Archbishop Islip, his uncle, made him his Vicar-General, and Dean of the Court of Arches, and procured his election to the See of Rochester in 1362.

He was translated to Worcester in 1364, and to Canterbury in 1368, but in consequence of his feeble health he lived much in seclusion, and died in 1374.

SIMON LANGHAM
(From his Tomb in Westminster Abbey)

Simon Langham

was born in Rutlandshire, and entered the Monastery of S. Peter's, Westminster, of which he became Abbot. In 1360 he was appointed Treasurer of England, Bishop of Ely in 1362, and for three years he also held the office of Chancellor. His administration was characterized by the determination with which he resisted papal encroachments. As Bishop he shewed equal vigour in correcting ecclesiastical abuses, and earned respect, though he may not have secured popularity. His translation to Canterbury took place in 1366.

In 1368 he incurred the displeasure of Edward III by accepting an appointment as Cardinal from Urban V without having obtained the Royal permission. Edward pronounced the See of Canterbury void, and seized the revenues. Langham betook himself to the papal court at Avignon, and was employed in negotiations between England, and France, and Flanders. He continued, however, to hold preferments in England, as Treasurer and Archdeacon of Wells, Archdeacon of Taunton, and Archdeacon of the West Riding.

Langham died in 1376, as he was about to return to England, and three years later his body was transferred to Westminster Abbey, which owed much to his great munificence.

Simon Islip

was probably born at Islip, on the Cherwell, and studied law at Merton College, Oxford. He held the benefices of Easton and Horncastle, and Prebends at Lincoln, Lichfield, and S. Paul's. He was Vicar-General to the Bishop of London, and Dean of Arches, and for three years Archdeacon of Canterbury.

He entered the service of Edward III, who procured his election to the Primacy in 1349.

The Black Death was then raging, and Islip found many parishes deserted by the clergy. He laboured earnestly to bring back the priests to the performance of their duties, and to enforce a higher standard of discipline. He also endeavoured to promote learning amongst the clergy, and to secure for them academic training, and founded a College at Oxford for the purpose, the situation of which is still marked by the Canterbury Quadrangle of Christ Church.

His death took place in 1366.

SEAL OF SIMON ISLIP

Thomas Bradwardine

was born at Chichester, and studied at the College which Walter de Merton had recently founded at Oxford. His learning as a theologian, a philosopher, and a mathematician, earned for him the title of Doctor Profundus.

The distinguishing mark of his teaching was the stress which he laid on the foreknowledge of GOD, and the need of divine grace, and this is referred to by Chaucer in his *Nun's Priest's Tale*.

He became Proctor of the University, and in that capacity took part in resisting the claim of certain unscrupulous people to farm the revenues of the Archdeaconry of Oxford, which was held by the Cardinal of S. Lucia, although he neglected to perform the duties of the office.

About 1335 Bradwardine was summoned to London to assist Richard de Bury, Bishop of Durham, in collecting books for his great library. Soon after this Bradwardine became Chancellor of S. Paul's, and was appointed Chaplain to Edward III. He accompanied the King during his progress through Flanders and Germany, and his campaign in France, and the victories of the English army were attributed by some to the influence of his teaching and his holy life.

In 1349 he was elected to the See of Canterbury, and after his consecration at Avignon he hastened back to England, where the Black Death was raging. But a few days after his arrival he died of the plague in London, and his body was removed to Canterbury, and laid in the Cathedral.

67

John Stratford

was born at Stratford-on-Avon, and educated at Merton College, Oxford, where he studied law. He became Archdeacon of Lincoln, and Dean of the Court of Arches, and in 1323 was consecrated Bishop of Winchester. From 1330 he was the Chancellor and chief adviser of Edward III, and was frequently employed in negotiations with France. In 1333 he was promoted to the Archbishopric of Canterbury.

His legal ability marked him out for the career of diplomacy and politics, with which his life was mainly occupied, but in his latter years he concerned himself more with ecclesiastical affairs.

He died in 1348.

TOMB OF JOHN STRATFORD
(In Canterbury Cathedral)

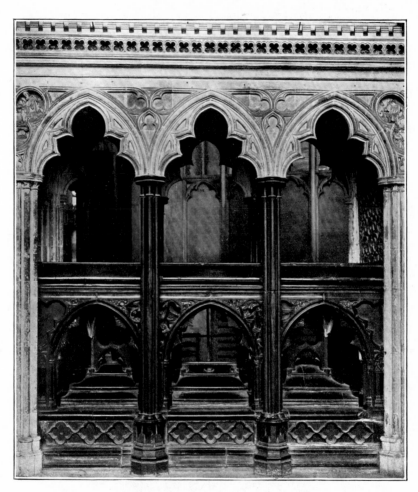

TOMB OF SIMON MEPEHAM

(In Canterbury Cathedral)

Simon Mepeham

was born in Kent, and studied at Oxford, and became noted for his knowledge of Holy Scripture. He was appointed Prebendary of Llandaff, and Canon of Chichester, and in 1328 was elected to the See of Canterbury.

Mepeham cared little for the secular ambitions which engrossed many of the clergy in his day. He earnestly desired to restore discipline in the Church, and to that end attempted a systematic visitation of his Province, which was keenly resented by some of his suffragans. He also gave great offence to the monks of S. Augustine's, by asking them to prove their claim to certain Kentish churches. The monks preferred to appeal to the Pope, and the decision was given against the Archbishop, who was called upon to pay to the monks costs to the amount of £700, under pain of excommunication. The Archbishop allowed the sentence to take effect, and it had not been removed at his death in 1333.

Walter Reynolds

was born at Windsor, and brought up at the Court of
Edward I, who appointed him governor of his son. On
the accession of Edward II he was made a Prebendary
of S. Paul's, Treasurer of the Exchequer, and Bishop
of Worcester, and in 1310 was appointed Chancellor.
Reynolds, who seems to have abetted Edward in his
follies and pleasures, was rewarded with the Primacy
in 1313. Although he made an attempt to remedy some
of the most glaring ecclesiastical abuses, his activity was
displayed in the field of politics, rather than in the
guidance of the Church.

During the troubles which marked Edward II's reign,
he first took part with the King, but transferred his
allegiance to Queen Isabella, and officiated at the
Coronation of Edward III, whilst Edward II yet
lived.

A few months later Reynolds died (1327).

TOMB OF WALTER REYNOLDS

(In Canterbury Cathedral)

SEAL OF ROBERT WINCHELSEY

Robert Winchelsey

so called from the town which was probably his birth-place, studied at Paris, becoming Rector of the University, and afterwards at Oxford, where he held the office of Chancellor. He was also appointed Archdeacon of Essex, and lectured on theology at S. Paul's, where he held a Prebend.

In 1294 he was consecrated to the See of Canterbury.

By insisting on his right as Metropolitan to carry out a visitation of his Province, and by rigorous attempts to enforce his claims of jurisdiction, he involved himself in frequent contests with the clergy, and the same uncompromising spirit also brought him into conflict with the King, for whilst profuse in his liberality to the poor, Winchelsey offered a determined resistance to the repeated demands of Edward I for subsidies to enable him to prosecute his warlike schemes. Fortified with the papal bull, *clericis laicos*, Winchelsey encouraged the clergy to refuse any further payments, and the struggle continued with little intermission till Edward prevailed upon Clement V to suspend Winchelsey from his functions (1306). The Archbishop was forced to leave the country, and only returned after the accession of Edward II, when he was reinstated, and exerted himself to emancipate the King from the domination of his unworthy favourites.

His death occured in 1313.

John Peckham

was brought up in Sussex, and educated at Lewes Priory, at Oxford, and in Paris. He entered the Franciscan Order, and was appointed theological lecturer in the papal schools at Rome. In 1279 Nicholas III nominated him to the See of Canterbury.

Peckham's assertion of ecclesiastical authority at the expense of the temporal power was resisted by Edward I, whilst his attempts to enforce his rights of jurisdiction involved him in contests with other Bishops, and the religious communities in his Province. At the same time it is clear that he was actuated by no desire for personal aggrandizement, but honestly sought to check ecclesiastical abuses, and especially the holding of livings in plurality. He also endeavoured to bring the Welsh Church into closer conformity with the customs of the Church in England.

He was a voluminous writer of poetry and treatises on theology and science.

His death occurred in 1292.

TOMB OF JOHN PECKHAM
(In Canterbury Cathedral)

SEAL OF ROBERT KILWARDBY

Robert Kilwardby

studied at the University of Paris, where he also taught grammar and logic, and wrote various grammatical and philosophical treatises. Having entered the Order of S. Dominic, he devoted himself thenceforth to the study of theology, and became Provincial Prior of the Dominicans.

In 1272 he was appointed by Gregory X to the See of Canterbury, and consecrated in 1273.

He displayed great energy in the visitation of his Province, held frequent Synods, was munificent in his gifts to the Dominican Order, and showed great care for the poor.

In 1278 he was appointed by Pope Nicholas III to the Cardinal Bishopric of Porto and Santa Rufina, and thereupon resigned the See of Canterbury, and went to Italy, where he died a year later.

Boniface

son of Thomas, Count of Savoy, became Bishop of
Belley, in Burgundy; and in 1241, through the influence
of his niece, Queen Eleanor, wife of Henry III, was
nominated to the See of Canterbury.

He did not, however, come to England till 1244, and
was present in the following year at the Council of
Lyons. There he was consecrated by Innocent IV,
but it was only in 1249 that he returned to England,
and was enthroned at Canterbury.

He showed little concern for the spiritual duties of
his office. His exactions and his overbearing behaviour,
combined with the fact that he was a foreigner, gave
great offence to the English. To his credit is his
attempt to free the Archiepiscopal See from debt, and
that, with all his faults, he is said to have been *pauperum
amator*.

During the Barons' War, Boniface seems to have
first made common cause with the English Bishops
against the exactions of Pope and King, but he drifted
more and more to the King's side. In 1262 he retired
to France, where he joined with the Papal Legate in
excommunicating the barons. On the triumph of the
Royalists in 1265 he returned to England.

Boniface was ordered by Pope Urban IV "either
to repair the buildings at Lambeth, or to build new
ones," and the present Early English Chapel of the
Palace is part of the work which he then undertook.

He died in 1270, whilst on a visit to his native land.

SEAL OF BONIFACE

SEAL OF EDMUND RICH

Edmund Rich

was born at Abingdon, and educated at Oxford and in Paris. For some years he remained at Oxford, first as a teacher of philosophy and mathematics, and then of theology, and in 1222 was appointed Treasurer of Salisbury Cathedral, which office he retained till he was promoted to the See of Canterbury in 1234. During the contest of Henry III with his barons, Edmund attached himself to the party which aimed at securing national independence, and freedom from the domination of Henry's foreign favourites. He also endeavoured to suppress many corrupt practices in the Church, and to this end his Constitutions were issued in 1236. The resentment he incurred led him to visit Rome, in order to lay his difficulties before the Pope, but he failed to secure any support from Gregory IX. Feeling his position to be intolerable, he retired to Pontigny, where he died in 1240. The memory of his pure and holy life attracted many worshippers to the shrine which marked the last resting-place of S. Edmund.

Richard le Grant

Also called Richard of Wethershed

was Chancellor of Lincoln from 1221 till 1229, when he
was consecrated to the Archbishopric of Canterbury by
the desire of Henry III and the Bishops.   Richard, however, was brought into conflict with the King and Hubert
de Burgh, whom he regarded as violating the rights of
his See.   He carried his cause to Rome, and the Pope
gave sentence in his favour, but on his homeward journey
he died in Umbria (1231).

SEAL OF RICHARD LE GRANT

TOMB OF STEPHEN LANGTON
(In Canterbury Cathedral)

Stephen Langton

though an Englishman by birth, studied at Paris, and remained there as a teacher of theology, till he was called to Rome by Innocent III, who made him a Cardinal. Both at Paris and Rome he was held in great honour for his learning and holiness, and in 1207 Innocent procured his election to the See of Canterbury. King John, however, declined to acknowledge him, and though the country was laid under an interdict, Langton laboured for six years to overcome the King's opposition before John yielded, and allowed him to come to England and enter upon his archiepiscopal functions. From the first Langton set himself to restrain the King's lawlessness, and to mediate between him and his aggrieved barons. The result of his efforts was the signing of the Magna Charta. But John succeeded in gaining over the Pope, and Langton was suspended from his archiepiscopal office, to which he was restored on the death of Innocent and of John. He continued to use his influence on behalf of peace and order in the State and in the Church; and at Osney in 1222, the Canons were promulgated known as the Constitutions of Stephen Langton.

He was the author of a large number of commentaries on the Bible, besides many other theological, historical, and poetical works.

His death occurred in 1228.

was the son of Norman parents who had settled in East Anglia. He grew up in the household of Ranulf de Glanville, his uncle, the Chief Justiciar of England, and held various offices under the Crown, besides the Deanery of York, before his consecration as Bishop of Salisbury in 1189. In the following year he accompanied Richard I to the Holy Land.

On his return from the Crusade, he took an active part in collecting the ransom demanded for Richard, and was elected at the instance of the King to the vacant See of Canterbury (1193). The same year he became Justiciar, and during Richard's prolonged absence the chief responsibility of government devolved upon him. It was no easy task to keep John in check, to provide for the national defence, and to adjust the taxation, yet Hubert, whilst ruling the State with diligence and prudence, was not unmindful of his ecclesiastical duties. He resigned the Justiciarship in 1198, but the following year accepted the office of Chancellor. How great an influence he continued to exercise in the State is shown by the words which John is said to have uttered, when tidings were brought to him, in 1205, of the death of the Archbishop: "Now, for the first time, am I truly King of England."

TOMB OF HUBERT WALTER

(In Canterbury Cathedral)

SEAL OF BALDWIN

was born at Exeter. He was appointed Archdeacon by the Bishop of Exeter, but resigned the office and entered the Cistercian Abbey at Ford, of which he became Abbot. In 1180 he was made Bishop of Worcester, and translated to Canterbury in 1185.

His pontificate was marked by a contest with the monks of Christ Church, Canterbury, which is of lasting interest, as having led to the residence of the Archbishops of Canterbury at Lambeth, in the teeth of papal opposition exerted through the agency of the monks of Christ Church. The contest arose not only from the monks' resentment of the stricter control which Baldwin endeavoured to exercise over them, but from the claim which they put forward to a right in the election of the Metropolitan himself, on the ground that when the Archbishop was also Prior of the Monastery, the election always lay with them. To escape from this interference, Baldwin formed the project of erecting a College of Secular Canons at Hackington, near Canterbury. This project was frustrated by a papal order, but Baldwin obtained a site at Lambeth, where he commenced the building of his College. The unfinished building was destroyed after his death, *vacante sede*, through the influence of the monks of Canterbury. A subsequent College, erected on additional ground purchased by exchange from the Cathedral body of Rochester by his successor, Hubert Walter, shared the same fate, but Hubert Walter succeeded in fixing his own residence on the same ground, close to the centre of the nation's life at Westminster, which has from that day been the home of the Archbishops.

In 1190 Baldwin, having preached in Wales on behalf of the Crusade, set out for the Holy Land, where he soon after died.

SEAL OF THOMAS BECKET

was born at Exeter. He was appointed Archdeacon by the Bishop of Exeter, but resigned the office and entered the Cistercian Abbey at Ford, of which he became Abbot. In 1180 he was made Bishop of Worcester, and translated to Canterbury in 1185.

His pontificate was marked by a contest with the monks of Christ Church, Canterbury, which is of lasting interest, as having led to the residence of the Archbishops of Canterbury at Lambeth, in the teeth of papal opposition exerted through the agency of the monks of Christ Church. The contest arose not only from the monks' resentment of the stricter control which Baldwin endeavoured to exercise over them, but from the claim which they put forward to a right in the election of the Metropolitan himself, on the ground that when the Archbishop was also Prior of the Monastery, the election always lay with them. To escape from this interference, Baldwin formed the project of erecting a College of Secular Canons at Hackington, near Canterbury. This project was frustrated by a papal order, but Baldwin obtained a site at Lambeth, where he commenced the building of his College. The unfinished building was destroyed after his death, *vacante sede*, through the influence of the monks of Canterbury. A subsequent College, erected on additional ground purchased by exchange from the Cathedral body of Rochester by his successor, Hubert Walter, shared the same fate, but Hubert Walter succeeded in fixing his own residence on the same ground, close to the centre of the nation's life at Westminster, which has from that day been the home of the Archbishops.

In 1190 Baldwin, having preached in Wales on behalf of the Crusade, set out for the Holy Land, where he soon after died.

Richard

a Norman by birth, entered the Monastery of Christ Church, Canterbury. He became Chaplain to Archbishop Theobald, and Prior of S. Martin's, Dover. He was elected, not without opposition, to the See of Canterbury, in succession to Thomas Becket, and was consecrated by Pope Alexander III in 1174. Whilst Richard's zeal in asserting what he considered to be the rights of his See brought him into conflict with the Archbishop of York and some of the monastic communities, he showed himself much more amenable to the King's wishes than his predecessor, and was regarded by Becket's followers as remiss in defending the liberties of the Church.

Richard died in 1184.

SEAL OF RICHARD

SEAL OF THOMAS BECKET

Thomas Becket

was born in London about 1118, and was educated at Merton Priory, and in Paris. At a later time he studied canon law at Bologna and Auxerre, after he had entered the service of Archbishop Theobald, who appointed him to the Archdeaconry of Canterbury.

In 1155 Henry II made him Chancellor of England. For seven years he remained the close friend of the King, sharing his counsels, fighting in his wars, and conducting his negotiations. But when against his wish he had been elected to the See of Canterbury, it became evident that the authority which Henry claimed to exercise was incompatible with Becket's conception of the duties of his new office. Opposition broke out again and again; Becket refused his consent to the Constitutions of Clarendon, and Henry retaliated by demanding the payment of large sums which he maintained were owing to him.

Becket fled to France to lay his complaint before the Pope, and threatened Henry with excommunication. The struggle continued for six years, and then, in defiance of Becket and the Pope, Henry caused his eldest son to be crowned by the Archbishop of York. The Pope proceeded to suspend the Archbishop of York and the other Bishops who had taken part in the ceremony.

Meanwhile Henry had consented that Becket should be restored to his See, and accordingly he returned to Canterbury in 1170.

Soon after he was visited by four knights from Henry's Court, who demanded with great violence the absolution of the suspended Bishops. The frightened followers of Becket drew him into the Cathedral. There his enemies found him, and struck him down, fearless to the last. Four years later Henry did public penance at his tomb.

L

Theobald

was born in Normandy, and entered the Monastery at Bec, of which he became Abbot in 1137. In the following year Stephen and Queen Matilda procured his election to the Primacy.

Theobald found himself placed in a position of singular difficulty, owing to the rival claims of Stephen and the Empress Matilda. Throughout he displayed remarkable courage, moderation, and faithfulness. Though he would not withdraw his fealty from Stephen, he effected the treaty by which the succession was peaceably secured to the son of the Empress. When the interests of the Church seemed to demand it, he showed himself capable of independence of action, and was rewarded for his fidelity by being appointed Papal Legate.

He was the founder of canonical jurisprudence in England, and attracted to his service many men of learning and ability. Foremost among these was Thomas Becket, to whom the Archbishop was much attached, and whom, on his recommendation, Henry II appointed to be his Chancellor.

Theobald's death took place in 1161.

William de Corbeuil

was born in France, and studied at Laon. He became a clerk of Bishop Ranulf Flambard, and a Canon of S. Augustine's. In 1123 he was promoted to the See of Canterbury.

A contest took place with the Archbishop of York, who refused to acknowledge the precedence claimed by William. They carried their case to the Pope, Honorius II, and William was appointed Papal Legate in England and Scotland. In 1130 he dedicated the new Cathedral of Canterbury begun by Lanfranc.

His death occurred in 1136.

Ralph d'Escures

sometimes called Ralph de Turbine, a Frenchman by birth, entered the Abbey of S. Martin at Séez, and was elected Abbot in 1089. Having been driven from his Monastery by Robert of Bellême, he came to England, and in 1108 was appointed to succeed his friend Gundulph, in the Bishopric of Rochester.

After the death of Anselm the See of Canterbury was vacant for five years, during which time Ralph administered the affairs of the diocese with great ability, and he was unanimously elected to the Archbishopric in 1114. The appointment gave great offence to the Pope, who considered that his sanction should have been obtained, and who beheld with displeasure the independent position of the English Church. Ralph was resolved to maintain the freedom of his Church, and also to assert the Primacy of his See, and refused to consecrate Thurstan, Archbishop-elect of York, unless he professed subjection to the See of Canterbury. Thurstan, however, appealed to Rome, and, after considerable delay, succeeded in obtaining consecration at the hands of Calixtus II.

Ralph died in 1122.

Anselm

was born at Aosta about 1033. He entered the
Monastery of Bec, which under Lanfranc had become a
centre of learning. Anselm succeeded Lanfranc as Abbot,
and in 1093, on a visit to England, he was compelled
by William Rufus to accept the Archbishopric of
Canterbury. William, however, continually thwarted
and harassed him, by plundering and oppressing the
Church, so that Anselm was driven to lay his difficulties
before the Pope. The appeal met with little success,
but on the death of William he was recalled by Henry I
and the voice of all the people. Fresh difficulties arose,
Henry desiring that Anselm should receive the investiture
at his hands, which Anselm declined unless this were
sanctioned by the Pope. He was inflexible in his
determination to protect the rights and liberties of
the Church, and finally the conflict was settled by a
compromise two years before his death, which took
place in 1109.

His honesty of purpose, his undaunted courage, his
saintly character, and above all, his great learning,
entitle him to be regarded as one of the chief glories
of the English Church. He was the author of many
theological and philosophical works, of which the most
famous was *Cur Deus Homo*.

Lanfranc

was born about 1005 at Pavia, where he was held in high esteem for his wisdom and learning. He moved to Normandy, and opened a school at Avranches, but feeling called to embrace a monastic life he entered the Monastery at Bec, which soon acquired great fame, and attracted many scholars, of whom Anselm was one. He was taken into the counsels of the Duke of Normandy, and travelled to Rome to procure a dispensation for the Duke's marriage, and to attend the Councils at which Berengar's views on the Eucharist were condemned. For four years he was Abbot of S. Stephen's at Caen, and in 1070 was consecrated Archbishop of Canterbury.

As Primate his efforts were largely directed to bringing the English Church into closer connection with the Churches of the Continent, by bestowing preferments on foreign ecclesiastics. He was also instrumental in procuring the separation of the spiritual from the temporal Courts. During William the Conqueror's absence from England, Lanfranc acted as his vicegerent. His vigorous administration was tempered by gentleness and liberality. In seven years he rebuilt his Cathedral, which had been burned in 1067.

His death took place in 1089.

STIGAND
(From " La Tapisserie de Bayeux ")

Stigand

was Chaplain to Cnut and Harald Harefoot, and adviser of Queen Emma. He was consecrated to the See of Elmham in 1043, and received the Bishopric of Winchester in 1047.

He was an adherent of Earl Godwine, and when Archbishop Robert fled from England on Godwine's return from exile, Stigand was appointed to succeed him (1052). The appointment was not recognized at Rome, and even in England his position was regarded as schismatical. In 1058 Benedict X consented to send him a pallium, but this only served to intensify the difficulties of his situation, for in 1059 Benedict was declared uncanonical, and was deposed.

After the death of King Harald, Stigand made his submission to the Conqueror, who insisted that the Archbishop should accompany him on his return to Normandy.

At William's request, in 1070 the Papal Legates were sent to England, and brought the following charges against Stigand: that he had usurped the Archbishopric during the lifetime of Robert, and used his pallium; that he had received his own pallium from an anti-pope; and that he had retained the Bishopric of Winchester after his appointment to Canterbury. Stigand was condemned, deprived of his dignities, and imprisoned at Winchester, where he died in 1072.

Robert

by birth a Norman, was appointed Abbot of Jumièges in 1037. When Eadward the Confessor was an exile in Normandy, he formed a friendship with Robert, who accompanied him on his return to England, and was given the Bishopric of London in 1044.

In 1051 Eadward insisted upon his translation to Canterbury, against the wishes of the Chapter, who had already elected Ælfric. The resentment aroused by this was increased by the use Robert made of his position to inflame the mind of the King against Earl Godwine, and to promote the interests of the foreigners, who filled many offices in Church and State. Godwine, however, proved in the end too strong for Robert, who was obliged to leave the country in 1052, and died at Jumièges in 1070.

Eadsige

Chaplain to King Cnut, and Bishop of S. Martin's outside Canterbury, was promoted to the Archbishopric in 1038.

He crowned Harthacnut, and officiated at the Coronation of Eadward the Confessor, which took place at Winchester in 1043.

Eadsige died in 1050.

Aethelnoth

called "the Good," a monk of Glastonbury, became Dean of Canterbury, and in 1020 was consecrated to the See of Canterbury by the Archbishop of York. He was the counsellor and close friend of King Cnut, working with him to make the English and the Danish settlers a united people.

He restored and beautified Canterbury Cathedral. His respect for the wishes of Cnut was shown in his refusal to crown Harald Harefoot.

Æthelnoth died in 1038.

Lyfing

was consecrated Bishop of Wells in 999, and was appointed by Æthelred the Unready to the See of Canterbury in 1013, a year marked by a fresh invasion of the Danes, who devastated the country far and wide.

Lyfing took part in framing the ecclesiastical laws which were enacted in the Witenagemot held in 1014.

In 1016 he crowned Eadmund Ironside, and Cnut in 1017. He began the restoration of Canterbury Cathedral, which had been partially destroyed by the Danes.

His death occurred in 1020.

Aelfric

entered the Monastery at Abingdon, became Bishop of Ramsbury in 990, and in 995 was translated to Canterbury.

He died in 1005.

Of the other events of his life, little can be related with certainty. In his will, which has been preserved, he made bequests of books and lands to S. Albans, which lends colour to the view that he was at one time Abbot of S. Albans. He left to the King his best ship, and armour for sixty men, a ship to the people of Wiltshire, and another to the people of Kent, and a cross to Bishop Ælfheah, who succeeded him.

Sigeric

was educated at Glastonbury, where he became a monk, and was elected Abbot of S. Augustine's, Canterbury, in 980. He was consecrated by Archbishop Dunstan to the See of Ramsbury in Wiltshire, and in 990 was translated to Canterbury. By his advice Æthelred the Unready attempted to purchase peace from the Danes for the sum of ten thousand pounds, a proceeding which only served to encourage fresh invasions.

Abbot Ælfric dedicated to him a book of homilies which he had translated from the Latin, requesting him to correct any blemishes or errors which he might detect. As, moreover, Sigeric bequeathed to his church a valuable collection of books, he seems to have been a man of learning.

He died in 994.

Ethelgar

was educated at Glastonbury under the care of Dunstan, and entered the Benedictine Monastery, founded by Bishop Æthelwold at Abingdon, and was appointed by him to be Abbot of Newminster. Though strictly observing the Benedictine Rule, Ethelgar did not adopt the harsh measures of Æthelwold towards the secular clergy.

He became Bishop of Selsey in 980, and in 988 was translated to Canterbury, and died after a brief archiepiscopate of scarcely more than one year.

Dunstan

the son of a West Saxon noble, was born in 924 or 925, and received his early education from the Irish monks who had settled at Glastonbury. After living for a time at the Court of King Æthelstan, he became a monk at Glastonbury, and devoted himself to the study of the Scriptures, and to prayer. At the same time he became skilled in the art of painting, and music, and in making church bells and organs.

Having been summoned to the Court of King Eadmund he became one of his chief councillors. The King, however, lent too ready an ear to malicious accusations which were brought against Dunstan, and dismissed him, but afterwards regretted his injustice, and made him Abbot of Glastonbury.

Soon after he became the treasurer and chief adviser of King Eadred and the Queen-mother; but powerful enemies drove him from the Court of King Eadwig, and he was obliged to take refuge in Flanders, till the accession of Eadgar, who recalled him and made him his chief minister. He was also appointed Bishop of Worcester and of London, and in 960 became Archbishop of Canterbury.

Amongst all those who have directed the government of the State whilst holding the highest office in the Church, Dunstan is entitled to a place of honour. He laboured with no small success to establish peace amongst the different peoples settled in England; he sought to raise the standard of monastic life; he built and endowed churches; he delighted in teaching, and encouraged the clergy to acquire knowledge that they might be the teachers of the nation.

After the brief reign of King Eadward had been closed by his tragic death, Dunstan took part in the Coronation of Æthelred. His death occurred in 988.

DUNSTAN

Odo

a Dane, was adopted by one of Ælfred's nobles, Æthelhelm, by whose means he was baptized, and educated for the priesthood. Æthelstan appointed him Bishop of Ramsbury, and in 942 he was promoted to Canterbury.

He repaired the Cathedral, and laboured earnestly to promote virtuous living amongst his people, admonishing the King and the nobles to show justice, the clergy to be diligent in teaching, and strict in their lives, and enjoining upon all the duty of keeping the Holy Days of the Church, of giving alms, and of living together in peace and charity.

He regarded with disapproval the marriage of King Eadwig with Ælfgifu, on the ground that they were too nearly related, and he caused them to be separated.

His death took place in 959.

Wulfhelm

was Bishop of Wells before his promotion, in 923, to the See of Canterbury.

King Æthelstan, who was crowned by him, refers to Wulfhelm and his other Bishops as his counsellors in the laws which he promulgated at Greetanlea.

Wulfhelm died in 942.

Athelm

is said to have been a monk of Glastonbury, and to have been raised to the episcopate in 909. In that year the two dioceses of Wessex were increased to five; Wells became the seat of one of the new bishoprics, and Athelm its first Bishop.

He was translated to Canterbury in 914, and died in 923.

Plegmund

a Mercian by birth, lived as a hermit in Cheshire, until he was summoned by King Ælfred to his Court, in order that he might take part in the great work which Ælfred had at heart, that of promoting learning amongst his people.

Ælfred, with the help of " Plegmund, my Archbishop," as he is styled in the preface, translated Pope Gregory's *Regula Pastoralis*, a copy of which was sent to every Bishop throughout the kingdom. The copy presented by the King to Plegmund is still preserved in the British Museum.

" Plegmund was chosen of GOD and of all the people Archbishop of Canterbury " in the year 890.

In 908 he consecrated the new Minster which Ælfred had founded at Winchester. During his pontificate the West Saxon episcopate was subdivided, and Plegmund is said to have consecrated seven Bishops in one day (909), of whom five were for Wessex.

His death took place in 914.

Ethelred

a monk of Canterbury, was appointed to the Archbishopric in 870. His pontificate derives lustre from
the conflicts and victory of King Ælfred, and the recep-
tion of a great multitude of Danes into the Church.

A mission was also sent by Ælfred to the Christians
of India in 883.

Ethelred died in 889.

Ceolnoth

Dean of Canterbury, was consecrated to the Archbishopric in 833. At the Council held at Kingston in 838, a perpetual alliance was concluded between the See of Canterbury and Ecgberht and Æthelwulf, the West Saxon Kings. Æthelwulf also granted a charter giving certain tithes to religious communities, who were in return to pray for the donors.

During the archiepiscopate of Ceolnoth, England was perpetually harassed by Danish raids, and it is conjectured that Ceolnoth was able to secure a certain measure of peace by coining a considerable amount of money with which he bought off the Danes.

He died in 870.

Feologild

was Abbot of a Kentish Monastery, and was elected to
the Archbishopric in 832, but died within three months
of his consecration.

Wulfred

was appointed to be the first Archdeacon of Canterbury by Archbishop Æthelheard, whom he succeeded in 805. Cenwulf, King of Mercia, availed himself of the weak condition of the Kentish kingdom to seize some of Wulfred's estates. The hostility between the King and the Archbishop was brought to the notice of the Pope, and Wulfred visited Rome once or twice, but no permanent reconciliation seems to have been effected.

Wulfred's coins are stamped with his own name and effigy, and do not, like the coins of Æthelheard, bear the name of the King of Mercia.

At the Council of Chelsea held in 816, eleven canons were enacted to regulate the services and the government of the Church.

Wulfred died in 832.

Archiepiscopal Coins

(ABOUT 1½ THE ACTUAL SIZE)

WULFRED

WULFRED

CEOLNOTH

CEOLNOTH

ETHELRED

Aethelheard

was appointed by King Offa to the See of Canterbury in support of the Mercian interest in 793. After the death of Offa, Kent attempted to shake off the Mercian supremacy, and Æthelheard fled from Canterbury, which drew upon him a rebuke from Alcuin for deserting his flock. Having been restored to his See, he obtained a decision from Pope Leo III annulling the right of Lichfield to be regarded as a Metropolitan See, and confirming the Primacy of Canterbury.

Æthelheard's death took place in 805.

Jaenberht

was Abbot of S. Augustine's, Canterbury. At the death
of Archbishop Bregowine, a contest took place between
the monks of S. Augustine's and the monks of Christ
Church with regard to his place of burial. Eventually
the monks of Christ Church retained the body, but they
elected Jaenberht to the Archbishopric (766).

Offa, King of Mercia, formed a scheme for abolishing
the primatial dignity of Canterbury by converting Lichfield into a Metropolitan See. He obtained the consent
of Pope Hadrian II, and Jaenberht was compelled to
relinquish several Dioceses which belonged to the Province of Canterbury.

He died in 791, and was buried in his old Monastery,
S. Augustine's.

Bregowine

was a Saxon by birth. The fame of the schools with which the labours of Theodore and Hadrian had enriched England drew Bregowine from his native land. In England his learning and holiness won for him high esteem, and in 759 he was called to occupy the chair of Augustine.

He died in 765.

Cuthbert

Abbot of Liminge, became Bishop of Hereford, and was translated to Canterbury in 741. He took part in the Synod of Clovesho, at which several canons were drawn up enjoining the due observance of Sunday, and admonishing the clergy to be diligent in baptizing and instructing their flocks, and in celebrating the sacred offices.

Cuthbert added to the Cathedral the Chapel of S. John the Baptist, which he desired should be the place of burial for himself and his successors, and here accordingly he was laid at his death in 758.

Nothelm

is described as "Archpriest of the Cathedral Church of S. Paul's, London." He supplied Bede with some of the information contained in his *Ecclesiastical History*, and travelled as far as Rome to inspect documents and procure copies of letters required for this purpose.

He was promoted to the See of Canterbury in 735, and about the same time the Archbishopric of York was re-established as a Metropolitan See.

He died in 740.

Tatwine

by birth a Mercian, entered the Monastery of Briudun, or Bredun, in Worcestershire.

In 731, when Tatwine was promoted to the See of Canterbury, Bede concluded his *Ecclesiastical History*. Of Tatwine he says that he was *vir religione et prudentia insignis, sacris quoque literis nobiliter instructus*.

His short archiepiscopate of three years seems to have been uneventful.

He died in 734.

Berctuald

(or Brihtwald)

was of Royal lineage, but little is known of his early
life. He is said by Bede to have been well versed in
Holy Scripture. About 670 he became Abbot of the
Monastery at Reculver, and in 693 was consecrated
Archbishop of Canterbury.

He appears to have governed the Church with
vigour and ability. New bishoprics were established in
Wessex during his pontificate. He presided at the
Council of Estrefeld in 702, at which Archbishop
Wilfrid was deposed and excommunicated; and three
years later at another Council, when it was arranged
that Wilfrid should receive the Bishopric of Hexham,
in place of the Archbishopric of York.

Berctuald died in 731.

Theodore

a native of Tarsus in Cilicia, was born about 602. Having studied in Athens he visited Rome, and whilst there was appointed by Pope Vitalian to the See of Canterbury, which had been vacant for four years. Theodore arrived in England in 669, and was well received everywhere. He was the first Archbishop whose authority the whole English Church was willing to acknowledge.

The aims which Theodore set before himself were the organization of the Church, and the encouragement of learning. He therefore consecrated Bishops to fill the vacant Sees, and subdivided the existing Dioceses.

Wilfrid, who at this time ruled all the Church north of the Humber, resisted the attempt to deprive him of any part of his Diocese ; but although on his appeal to Rome, the papal decision was given in his favour, Theodore proceeded with the subdivision of the Northumbrian episcopate. Shortly before his death he was reconciled to Wilfrid, who was restored to his See.

The diocesan system which Theodore sought to establish was accepted by a Synod of the united English Church held at Hertford in 673. Another Synod held at Hatfield in 680 affirmed the adhesion of the English Church to the Catholic Faith.

The enlightened zeal of Theodore made learning to flourish in England. Under his direction, and with the able help of Hadrian and Benedict Biscop, seminaries were founded at many of the Monasteries.

Theodore died in 690.

Deusdedit

the first Saxon Archbishop of Canterbury, was known as Frithona till his consecration in 655.

The See of Canterbury seems at this time to have been passing through a period of comparative obscurity, for during the nine years of the pontificate of Deusdedit, all the new English Bishops, with one exception, were consecrated by Celtic or foreign Bishops.

The conference at Whitby was held in 664. Deusdedit does not appear to have been present, and his death took place a few months later.

Honorius

a Roman by birth, was of the number of those chosen by Gregory the Great for the evangelization of England. In 627 he was consecrated by Paulinus to the See of Canterbury. When Paulinus, after the death of Eadwine, fled before the storm which broke over the Church in Northumbria, he was received by Honorius, and appointed to the Bishopric of Rochester.

Felix the Burgundian was sent forth by Honorius, and perhaps consecrated by him as the first Bishop of East Anglia.

Honorius died in 653.

Justus

by birth a Roman, was one of the missionaries who came to England at the request of Augustine in 601. He was appointed to be the first Bishop of Rochester. When persecution broke out after the death of Æthelberht, he fled to Gaul, but a year later he was reinstated in his bishopric, which he governed with diligence and care till, in 624, he became Archbishop of Canterbury.

The most notable event of his brief archiepiscopate was the evangelization of Northumbria. Paulinus was consecrated by Justus to be the first Archbishop of York, and within two years King Eadwine was baptized with many of his people, in a little church which he had built at York, on the ground where now York Minster stands. The good news was conveyed to Justus not long before his death, which is believed to have taken place in 627.

Mellitus

was sent to England in 601 by Pope Gregory in response to an appeal from Augustine for a fresh band of missionaries.

He was commissioned by Gregory to convey the pallium to Augustine, together with a present of books, and "all things which were needed for worship and the ministry of the Church."

When London once more became the seat of a bishopric, Mellitus was chosen by Augustine to be Bishop of the See, and the Church of S. Paul was founded as its Cathedral.

He was driven from London by the heathen sons of Sebert, in consequence of his refusal to give them the sacramental bread unless they consented to be baptized. He fled to Gaul, but was recalled by Laurentius, upon whose death in 619 he succeeded to the Archbishopric of Canterbury, and died in 624. Of the last years of his life scarcely anything is known.

Laurentius

was one of the band of missionaries who accompanied Augustine from Rome, and succeeded him as Archbishop in 604.

He endeavoured, without much success, to conciliate the ancient Church of Britain and Scotland.

After the death of King Æthelberht, a heathen reaction set in, and Bede relates that Laurentius was only deterred from leaving the country by a vision of S. Peter, who rebuked and chastised him. King Eadbald, to whom he showed his stripes, thereupon renounced idolatry, and was baptized, and the persecution came to an end.

Laurentius died in 619.

CANTERBURY CATHEDRAL

Canterbury Cathedral

After Augustine had established his episcopal seat at Canterbury he "recovered therein a church which he learned had been built by the ancient Roman Christians, and he hallowed it in the name of our Holy Saviour." In these words Bede describes the founding of Canterbury Cathedral, but of the church built by Augustine no trace is now visible.

It was set on fire by the Danes in 1011, and another conflagration took place in 1067, after which it was entirely rebuilt by Lanfranc and his successors. The choir was again destroyed by fire in 1174, and William of Sens was chosen to restore the east end; this work was completed by another William, an Englishman, in 1184.

In 1220 Becket's remains were removed from the crypt, and translated with great pomp to the shrine erected to receive them in the Trinity Chapel. The shrine and the body were entirely destroyed by command of Henry VIII.

The rebuilding of the nave was begun by Simon Sudbury in 1378, and completed in 1411.

The south-west tower, which was begun by Archbishop Chicheley, and the great central tower (known as the Angel Steeple) were added before the close of the fifteenth century.

The north-west tower was rebuilt in 1831.

Oxford

A. R. MOWBRAY AND CO. LTD., CHURCH PRINTERS